Communicate!

Documentaries

Kelly Rodgers

Consultant

Laura Waters, M.A.
Professor of Communications

Publishing Credits

Rachelle Cracchiolo, M.S.Ed., *Publisher*
Conni Medina, M.A.Ed., *Managing Editor*
Nika Fabienke, Ed.D., *Series Developer*
June Kikuchi, *Content Director*
Seth Rogers, *Editor*
Michelle Jovin, M.A., *Assistant Editor*
Lee Aucoin, *Senior Graphic Designer*

TIME For Kids and the TIME For Kids logo are registered trademarks of TIME Inc. Used under license.

Image Credits: p.4 Kristin Callahan/ACE/Newscom; pp.6–7 Eddie Gerald/Alamy Stock Photo; p.8 Derek Storm/Everett Collection/Alamy Live News; p.10 (inset) Entertainment Pictures/Alamy Stock Photo; p.12 (inset) Everett Collection, Inc./Alamy Stock Photo; pp.12–13 ZUMA Press, Inc./Alamy Stock Photo; p.14 (inset) Nancy Stone/MCT/Newscom; pp.14–15 Moviestore collection Ltd/Alamy Stock Photo; pp.16–17 Atlaspix/Alamy Stock Photo; p.17 (inset) Kris Connor/Getty Images for The Weinstein Company; pp.18, 19 Illustrations by Timothy J. Bradley; pp.22–23 Robert Gilhooly/Alamy Stock Photo; p.22 (inset) Featureflash Photo Agency/Shutterstock.com; p.26 Kris Connor/Getty Images for The Weinstein Company; p.30 (inset) Richard Levine/Alamy Stock Photo; pp.30–31 ZUMA Press, Inc./Alamy Stock Photo; p.40 J. Howard Miller/ZUMA Press/Newscom; all other images from iStock and/or Shutterstock.

Library of Congress Cataloging-in-Publication Data

Names: Rodgers, Kelly author.
Title: Communicate! : documentaries / Kelly Rodgers.
Description: Huntinton Beach, CA : Teacher Created Materials, 2017. | Includes index.
Identifiers: LCCN 2017023523 (print) | LCCN 2017034886 (ebook) | ISBN 9781425854621 (eBook) | ISBN 9781425849863 (pbk.)
Subjects: LCSH: Documentary films--History and criticism--Juvenile literature.
Classification: LCC PN1995.9.D6 (ebook) | LCC PN1995.9.D6 R5795 2017 (print)
| DDC 070.1/8--dc23
LC record available at https://lccn.loc.gov/2017023523

Teacher Created Materials

5301 Oceanus Drive
Huntington Beach, CA 92649-1030
http://www.tcmpub.com

ISBN 978-1-4258-4986-3

© 2018 Teacher Created Materials, Inc.

Table of Contents

Playing a Vital Role

Have you ever watched a film that made you think about the lives of others? Or one that made you want to help solve a problem? If so, the film may have been a documentary. These films tell stories about real people and real events. Sometimes, they focus on nature or life in the past. Often, they focus on rights.

The rights of people and animals are the theme of many documentaries. Every person has rights. These are called *human rights*. Making sure animals receive **humane** treatment is called *animal rights*. Documentary **filmmakers** can play key roles in making sure human rights and animal rights are protected. They educate and inspire viewers. They urge them to take action.

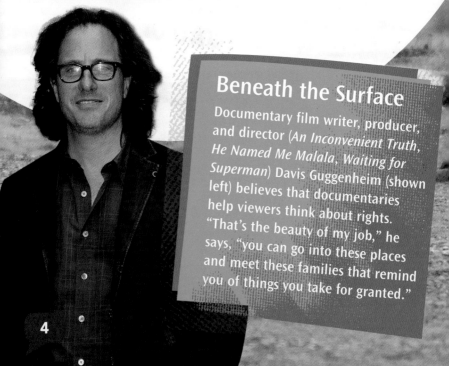

Beneath the Surface

Documentary film writer, producer, and director (*An Inconvenient Truth, He Named Me Malala, Waiting for Superman*) Davis Guggenheim (shown left) believes that documentaries help viewers think about rights. "That's the beauty of my job," he says, "you can go into these places and meet these families that remind you of things you take for granted."

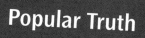

Popular Truth

An Inconvenient Truth is the most popular documentary film ever made. It fights for the rights of all living creatures by making people aware of **climate change**. The film also inspires people to take care of the environment.

The Language of Film

Films are a type of **visual art**. They tell stories through images and film language. Film language is the way all of the sights and sounds of a film impact its overall message. Viewers interpret this language to understand the film's message.

Distinctions

Documentaries, or nonfiction films, are a distinct film **genre**. They record real life. They show real struggles. Films about rights show how humans and animals suffer when their rights are not protected. Humans cannot always stand up for their own rights. Animals cannot speak out for theirs. Documentaries show people how they can help fight for the rights of others.

A Global Declaration

The Universal Declaration of Human Rights (UDHR) was released in 1948 by the United Nations. Though old, it is still an important document. It spells out basic rights for all humans. The UDHR states that all people "are born free and equal in dignity and rights." It includes the rights to life, freedom, and equal protection of the law.

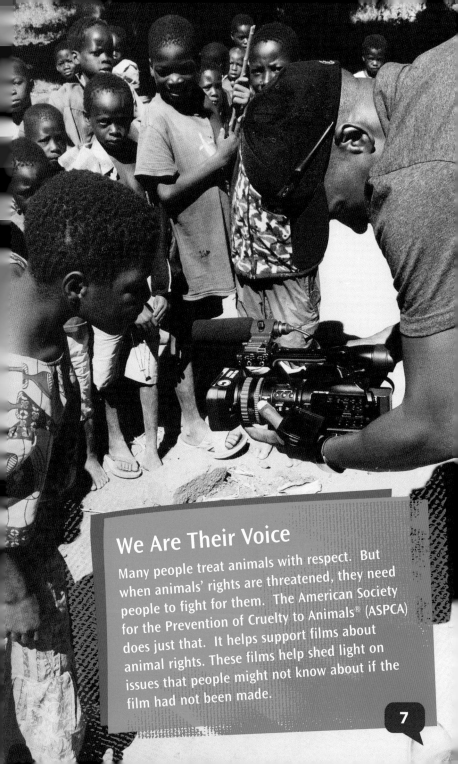

We Are Their Voice

Many people treat animals with respect. But when animals' rights are threatened, they need people to fight for them. The American Society for the Prevention of Cruelty to Animals® (ASPCA) does just that. It helps support films about animal rights. These films help shed light on issues that people might not know about if the film had not been made.

Common Ground

Many documentaries deal with rights. Some films focus on children's rights. These films may focus on bullying in schools or children who have to deal with hunger. Other films shed light on **racism** or **gender discrimination**. And still others show how humans mistreat animals.

Documentaries about rights have certain things in common. They tell stories about people who are fighting to end injustice. They show people who have dealt with these issues firsthand. They show the viewer that anyone can make a difference. And they use film language to **convey** their meanings.

Promoting Love

Lizzie Velasquez (shown left) was born with a disorder that causes her to look different from most people. She was bullied for most of her life. Now, she fights against bullying. Lizzie started her own YouTube channel, which she uses to promote love and hope. The documentary, *A Brave Heart: The Lizzie Velasquez Story*, tells about her life.

Two Sides of the Story

The Elephant in the Living Room focuses on the problems with keeping wild animals as pets. The film shows the struggle to protect the rights of owners and animals. One image in the film shows a lion named Lambert caged in a horse trailer. Seeing a wild animal trapped in a small area stuck in the minds of many viewers.

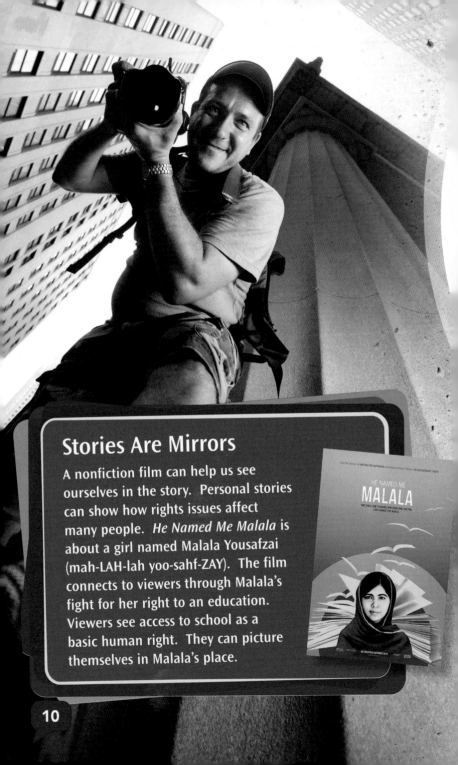

Stories Are Mirrors

A nonfiction film can help us see ourselves in the story. Personal stories can show how rights issues affect many people. *He Named Me Malala* is about a girl named Malala Yousafzai (mah-LAH-lah yoo-sahf-ZAY). The film connects to viewers through Malala's fight for her right to an education. Viewers see access to school as a basic human right. They can picture themselves in Malala's place.

HE NAMED ME
MALALA

Shots and Camera Angles

Filmmakers use shots and camera angles to tell their stories. A shot is a single image (like a photograph) that the camera records. When a group of shots are strung together, they create a scene. Many scenes together form a film. In that way, is it similar to a flipbook.

There are different types of shots and camera angles. Each one can convey a unique meaning. For example, a close-up shot of a child's face can make viewers feel attached to the child. A long shot of a child standing alone in a street can make viewers feel sorry for the child. The way the camera is angled can mean things, too. For instance, when a camera looks down on a person in a film, viewers feel like they have the power. When the camera looks up at someone, viewers feel respect for him or her. Filmmakers use these methods to make their **themes** clear.

Setting It Up

A Place at the Table documents the tragic stories of American children who do not have enough to eat. The film opens with some **establishing shots**. These shots show various cities and towns across the United States. They help prepare viewers for the message of the film.

Light and Sound

Filmmakers use special techniques to help make the message of their documentaries clear. These techniques help the viewers grasp the filmmakers' issues. One of these techniques is to use lighting and music to set certain moods. Dark lighting creates a scared or tense mood. Bright lighting creates a hopeful mood. The same is true for sounds. Lights and sounds can make viewers feel things that they might not otherwise.

Narration, or voice-over, is another technique. Voice-overs give the viewers information that they might not know. This helps viewers get a deeper understanding of the events on the screen.

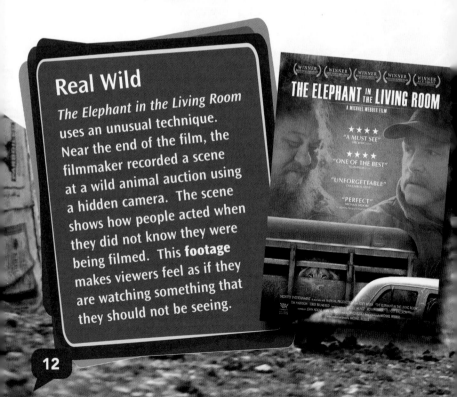

Real Wild

The Elephant in the Living Room uses an unusual technique. Near the end of the film, the filmmaker recorded a scene at a wild animal auction using a hidden camera. The scene shows how people acted when they did not know they were being filmed. This **footage** makes viewers feel as if they are watching something that they should not be seeing.

Images Speak Loudly

In *He Named Me Malala*, Malala's voice-overs tell facts about her life and education. At the same time, viewers see a shot of a street in her home country of Pakistan. The street has been blocked. The filmmaker uses the visual to act as a metaphor that shows that the road to equal education in Pakistan is also blocked.

Malala Yousafzai (center), her father Ziauddin (left), and Syrian refugees walk through a Syrian refugee camp.

In Their Own Words

Documentary films have **subjects**, not characters. Sometimes, the subject acts as the film's narrator. This technique gives the film a personal point of view. Subjects help viewers see the world through their eyes. This makes the issue feel real for viewers.

Filmmakers also interview their subjects. This technique lets subjects tell their stories in their own words. They can express their thoughts and feelings. Interviews can take place over hours or even days. Before the interviews make it into the film, filmmakers may have to edit them to make them shorter. In this way, viewers only see what the filmmaker wants them to see.

Balanced

Hoop Dreams tells the story of Arthur Agee and William Gates (shown above). The film follows them when they were boys as they fought racism and tried to make careers playing basketball. The filmmakers interviewed the boys, their families, and their friends. These interviews help balance the factual and emotional sides of the film.

Arthur Agee

Real Talks

In *Hoop Dreams*, the filmmakers show old photos of Agee's family. His mother provides a voice-over about the hard life Agee has faced. That works to create a connection between the boys and the viewers. After that, there is a scene of Agee playing basketball. This shows that basketball can pave the way to a better life.

Real or Created?

Some real events are hard to understand. Some filmmakers put words on the screen to help explain events. The text helps move the story along and provides facts. The text can also summarize events that the filmmaker chose to leave out or did not film.

Many nonfiction films use old photos and news articles, too. These tools remind viewers that they are seeing real events. Some films use **reenactments**. Filmmakers can shape these scenes to fit the message of their films. Blurred images and lighting changes are others signs that tell viewers that scenes are reenactments.

Real or Reenacted?

In *Mighty Times: The Children's March*, filmmakers used reenactments of civil rights marches. After the film was released, some viewers did not like the reenactments. They thought the filmmakers should have used actual footage of the marches. But filmmakers argued that they could make images clearer if they reenacted them.

Oprah Winfrey in a civil rights reenactment from the 2014 movie, *Selma*.

Say No to Bullying

Bully follows the lives of five children who are frequently bullied. At different points in the film, photographs and videos of the children when they were younger appear on the screen. These scenes serve to make viewers want to protect these young children from harm.

IT'S TIME TO TAKE A STAND

BULLY

Cracking the Code

Understanding film language helps viewers make sense of what they see. Filmmakers craft each shot to make sure they communicate specific ideas or emotions. Here are some important questions to think about while watching a documentary:

> **camera angle**—Where is the camera positioned, and how does that relate to the subject?

75 FT.

65 FT.

60 FT.

> **depth of focus**—Who/what is closest to the camera? Who/what is farthest from the camera?

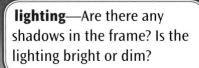

lighting—Are there any shadows in the frame? Is the lighting bright or dim?

framing—Who/what is in the shot? Who/what is not in the shot? Where are the subjects placed?

music—Is there music playing? How does it affect what you think? Is there silence? How does what you do or do not hear change what you think?

camera movement—How does the camera move in each shot? Does the camera move quickly or slowly? Does the movement make you think or feel anything?

19

A Noble Aim

Documentaries have many layers. Film language can help reveal the purpose of the film. Usually, the purpose is to educate viewers about a topic. But many films have more than one purpose. They may also seek to inspire viewers to take action.

Real Power

In 2004, *Super Size Me* showed the negative effects of eating too much fast food. The director of the film, Morgan Spurlock, ate nothing but McDonald's for an entire month. By the end of the month, Spurlock had gained 25 pounds (11.34 kilograms) and developed serious health problems. Viewers were shocked by what they saw. People began to look at fast food in a new light.

All around the world, people fight for their rights. People may hear about a human or animal rights issue. They may see a news program or read an article. But there are still some things that remain unknown. Many nonfiction films focus on these lesser-known events. By shining a light on these issues, filmmakers hope they can make their subjects' lives better.

Food Deserts

A Place at the Table talks about "food deserts." A food desert is a place where fresh food is not available. According to the film, over 23 million Americans live in these places.

Nonfiction films are windows to the world. Films that fight for the rights of others are unique windows. They give viewers a glimpse of the larger world around them. They offer ideas for ways to fight for **social change** and to protect rights. They attempt to motivate viewers to change the way they see the world.

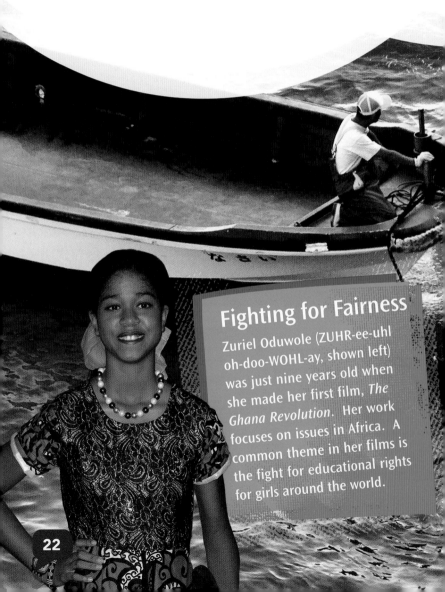

Fighting for Fairness

Zuriel Oduwole (ZUHR-ee-uhl oh-doo-WOHL-ay, shown left) was just nine years old when she made her first film, *The Ghana Revolution*. Her work focuses on issues in Africa. A common theme in her films is the fight for educational rights for girls around the world.

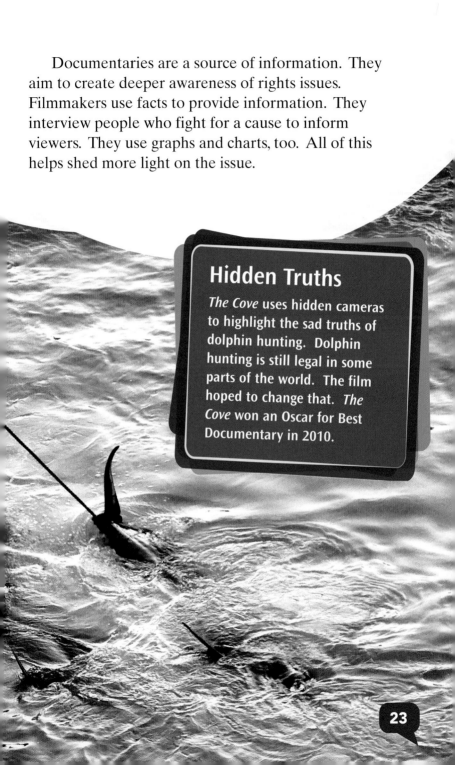

Documentaries are a source of information. They aim to create deeper awareness of rights issues. Filmmakers use facts to provide information. They interview people who fight for a cause to inform viewers. They use graphs and charts, too. All of this helps shed more light on the issue.

Hidden Truths

The Cove uses hidden cameras to highlight the sad truths of dolphin hunting. Dolphin hunting is still legal in some parts of the world. The film hoped to change that. *The Cove* won an Oscar for Best Documentary in 2010.

A Source of Inspiration

Documentaries inspire viewers. These films show why it is important to stand up for others. They teach people to have **compassion**. They also help people stay informed and introduce them to rights issues.

People who learn more about rights issues are more likely to take a stand for others. Documentaries encourage viewers to do so. These films do this by showing that all humans are connected. Life is not only about personal needs. It is also about caring for each other. Fighting for the rights of others should be part of every life.

Work Together

A Brave Heart: The Lizzie Velasquez Story educates and inspires. The filmmakers show Lizzie lobbying in Washington, DC, for the Safe Schools Improvement Act. This law protects victims of school bullying. Lizzie says, "Let's be heard together. Together, let's make a difference."

THERE IS NO PLANET B

Documentaries that fight for others' rights also aim to persuade viewers. They try to convince viewers that the issues are important. These films hope that those who watch will relate to their subjects. The goal is to get viewers to change how they see the subjects of the films. If the film is successful, then viewers might get involved.

Anyone can fight to protect the rights of others. Age, strength, and knowledge do not matter. Ordinary people can help ensure the rights of others. Documentaries inspire audiences to make change happen.

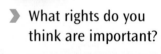

THINK LINK

❯ What rights do you think are important?

❯ How would you use a documentary to showcase your issue?

❯ Which film tools and techniques do you think have the biggest impact on viewers?

Filmmaker Lee Hirsh walks with Kelby Johnson after a screening of *Bully*.

A Global Influence

Kelby Johnson is one of the students featured in the documentary *Bully*. Kelby has faced bullying for many years. Even so, she refuses to move to a different school. In the film, she tells her parents, "If I leave, they win." Kelby's story has inspired many viewers.

A United Pursuit

The Universal Declaration of Human Rights (UDHR) is a document that forms the basis for global human rights law. Nearly every nation in the world agrees with the UDHR, yet human rights abuses still occur.

Some Universal Human Rights

Every person has the right to:

- equality.
- life, liberty, and personal security.
- be recognized as a person under the law.
- equality under the law.
- fair and capable judges to uphold their rights.
- a fair and public hearing.
- be considered innocent until proven guilty.
- free movement.
- protection while in another country.
- a nationality and the freedom to change it.
- marriage and family.

- own property.
- peaceful assembly and association.
- participate in government and elections.
- social security.
- desirable work and to join trade unions.
- rest and leisure.
- adequate living standards.
- education.
- participate in cultural life and responsibilities in the community.
- social order.
- freedom of thought, conscience, and religion.
- freedom of opinion and information.

Every person has freedom from:

- discrimination.
- slavery.
- torture.
- arrest and exile without reason.
- interference with privacy, family, home, and correspondence.

The Key Factor

Filmmakers make documentaries with viewers in mind. The audience fulfills the purpose of the film. They respond to the film language. Filmmakers count on this response. They create content to reach viewers.

Changing Views

Nonfiction films tell stories that challenge viewers. These stories make viewers question what they think, know, and feel. The audience responds to the subjects of the film. The issues, struggles, people, and animals are all subjects. These films inspire viewers to think about how people and animals are treated around the world.

Don't Super Size Me

When viewers saw the poor effects that too much fast food had on Spurlock in *Super Size Me*, they took action. People demanded that McDonald's serve healthier options. Six weeks after the film was released, McDonald's started to phase out its "super size" option.

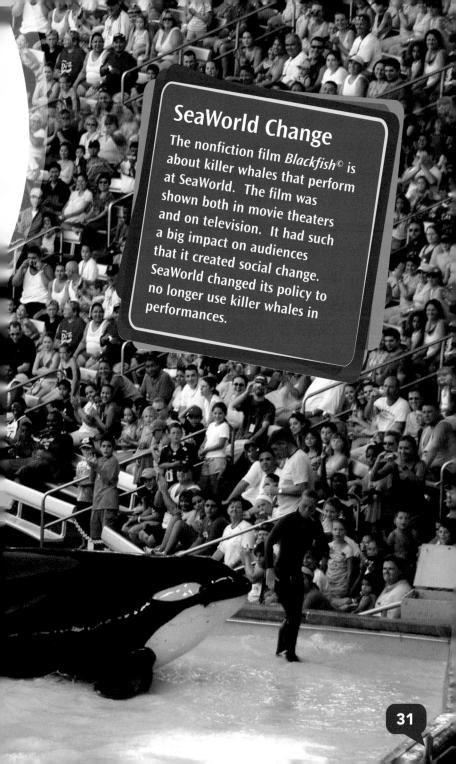

SeaWorld Change

The nonfiction film *Blackfish*© is about killer whales that perform at SeaWorld. The film was shown both in movie theaters and on television. It had such a big impact on audiences that it created social change. SeaWorld changed its policy to no longer use killer whales in performances.

Audience Appeal

Filmmakers know how to connect viewers with issues. They know how to make people think and feel certain ways. Filmmakers use camera angles and music. They use lighting and voice-overs. They do all of this to connect with viewers.

Each image and scene in a nonfiction film is an **appeal**. Filmmakers use appeals to try to persuade viewers to shift their beliefs, feelings, and thoughts. Sometimes, documentaries are hard to watch because they show so much pain. That works as an appeal to viewers to help make a change.

Sit-In

The Dream Is Now follows the lives of four **undocumented** children. In one scene, one of the subjects, Erika, is arrested. She had just staged a **sit-in** at a senator's office. Erika is appealing to the senator to take her rights issues seriously. At the same time, she is appealing to the film's viewers to do the same.

A Heart for Service

Another subject in *The Dream Is Now* is Alejandro. He has spent his whole life wanting to be a Marine. But because he is undocumented, he cannot serve in the military. When Alejandro speaks to filmmakers about his situation, he begins to cry. "Why try if I can't get there, or if I will never get there?" he asks.

Filmmakers use three main types of appeals: *ethos, logos,* and *pathos.* When all three are used together in an effective way, filmmakers can connect with viewers in meaningful ways.

Ethos appeals to the beliefs of the viewers. Do the images and people speaking have authority? Is the message in the film realistic?

Logos appeals to viewers' reason. Does the film have real facts? Is the message clear?

Pathos appeals to viewers' emotions. Does the film inspire them? Do the images make them feel a certain way? Does the story inspire them to take action?

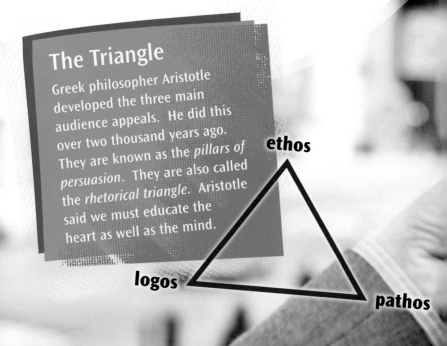

The Triangle

Greek philosopher Aristotle developed the three main audience appeals. He did this over two thousand years ago. They are known as the *pillars of persuasion.* They are also called the *rhetorical triangle.* Aristotle said we must educate the heart as well as the mind.

ethos

logos

pathos

Women in Media

Miss Representation is a film about the way in which women are shown in the **media**. The first shot of the film shows a quote from author Alice Walker: "The most common way people give up their power is by thinking they don't have any." The next shot shows data about how much time teenagers spend interacting with media. The first quote from the author appeals to viewers' pathos and ethos. The data appeals to viewers' logos.

A Better Chance

Audience members have a purpose. As they watch a documentary, they question what they see and hear. Viewers interpret the message in the images and respond to the appeals in the film. The viewer can be a key factor in protecting the rights of others.

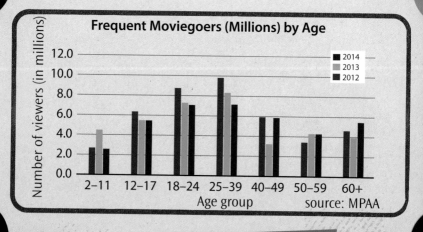

Frequent Moviegoers (Millions) by Age

Who's Watching?

Filmmakers know they need to reach certain audiences with their content, messages, and presentations. People between the ages of 18 and 39 make up the largest **demographic** of moviegoers. Filmmakers know that fact. So they try to appeal to that age group. They keep those people in mind when they are crafting the language of their films.

Documentaries are meaningless without an audience. When viewers respond to these films, there is a better chance of finding solutions to the issues in question. This is how change takes place. Viewers respond by standing up and speaking out. They respond by joining the fight for the rights of others.

STOP! THINK...

Filmmakers need an audience to connect with their message to be effective. Use the graph on the previous page to help you answer the following questions:

> What age group will most filmmakers try to appeal to?

> How does the audience fulfill the filmmaker's purpose?

> Why does the number of moviegoers in each age group change from year to year?

DIG DEEPER

What Can You Do?

Nonfiction filmmakers want your help. They want you to stay informed, donate money, and get involved with issues. Many organizations need young people to help. Social change often begins with youth.

Do you care about injustice around the world? Try joining a global movement of over 5 million young people making positive change with rights issues.

www.dosomething.org/

Are the rights of animals and the environment your passion? Help protect those without a voice.

www.onegreenplanet.org/

Does your school support the Safe Schools Improvement Act? Learn more about this campaign to stop bullying and make your voice heard by writing to politicians.

www.hrc.org/

Do you know of issues in your community? Make a documentary of your own to help protect the rights of others. Be sure to decide on the purpose, create the language, and find how you will appeal to your specific demographic before filming.

www.minimoviemakers.com

A Better Place

Documentary filmmakers have many roles. They are reporters and **advocates**. They are **activists** and explorers. But most important, they are storytellers. They aim to make people aware of issues. By making these films, they fight for the rights of others.

Documentaries speak through images and film language tools. They appeal to the viewers' emotions. After the film is over, it is up to audience members to create meaning from the film's language and purpose. It is then that documentaries fulfill their purpose of causing social change to happen.

Seeing Change

Miss Representation leads viewers to fight for change. Some people use Twitter™ to point out when they see bad images of women in media. Others send out weekly e-mails. These e-mails keep subscribers up-to-date on things they can do to help change how women are shown in media.

We Can Do It!

What It Means

After seeing *An Inconvenient Truth*, 9 out of 10 viewers said it made them more aware of climate change. People saw the impact climate change could have on both humans and animals. Since the film's release, new forms of energy, such as solar and wind, have come into use. And over 1 million electric cars have been sold around the world.

Glossary

activists—people who use or support strong actions to change things

advocates—people who support causes

appeal—a serious request for help or support

climate change—changes in Earth's weather patterns

compassion—a feeling of wanting to help another person or animal

convey—to make something known to someone

demographic—a group of people that has a set of qualities in common

establishing shots—types of film shots that tell viewers where and when the scene is taking place

filmmakers—people, such as producers or directors, who make movies

footage—scenes recorded on film or video

gender discrimination—the practice of unfairly treating a person or group of people differently based on whether they are male or female

genre—a certain category or type of art

humane—kind or gentle to animals or people

lobbying—trying to influence government officials to make decisions for or against something

media—radio stations, TV stations, newspapers, and films through which information is delivered to the public

racism—unfair treatment of people because of their race

reenactments—events that have been acted out again

sit-in—a protest where a group of people sit or stay in a place and refuse to leave

social change—a shift in the way people act and think about a particular topic

subjects—people or things shown in works of art

themes—the main subjects described or discussed

undocumented—a person who does not have the official documents that are needed to enter, live in, or work in a country legally

visual art—a work of art that relies on sight, such as drawing, painting, and film

Index

Check It Out!

Books

International Amnesty. 2015. *We Are All Born Free: The Universal Declaration of Human Rights in Pictures.* Francis Lincoln Ltd.

McLaughlin, Danielle. 2016. *That's Not Fair! Getting to Know Your Rights and Freedoms.* CitizenKid.

Videos

An Inconvenient Truth. 2006. Lawrence Bender Productions and Participant Media. PG.

A Place at the Table. 2012. Motto Pictures and Participant Media. PG.

Mighty Times: The Children's March. 2004. HBO Family. NR.

Super Size Me. 2004. The Con and Kathbur Pictures. PG.

The Elephant in the Living Room. 2010. NightFly Entertainment. PG.

Websites

Kids Go Global. www.kidsgoglobal.net

Kid World Citizen. www.kidworldcitizen.org/

Mini Movie Makers. www.minimoviemakers.com

Youth for Human Rights: Making Human Rights a Global Reality. www.youthforhumanrights.org/

Try It!

Imagine you are a documentary filmmaker. Choose an issue that is important to you and plan your film.

★ Which issue will you focus on?

★ Who will be your target audience? Be sure to keep that demographic's interests in mind when you choose a topic.

★ Research your topic. Gather data that shows why your issue is important.

★ Draw a scene from your film and label subjects, landmarks, and other important things.

★ Write a voice-over for the first scene of your film. Be sure to use words that will grab viewers' attention.

About the Author

Kelly Rodgers lives in Georgia with her family. She teaches middle school and high school history. When Rodgers is not teaching, she likes to read historical fiction novels. Rodgers also likes learning about the lives of the presidents. During summers, she likes traveling to new places. Rodgers enjoys seeing how other people live around the world. She does this in part by watching some of her favorite documentaries.